To Catch A Lightning Bug

Jhane Tutt

BookLeaf Publishing

India | USA | UK

Presentation by *BookLeaf Publishing*

Web: www.bookleafpub.com

E-mail: info@bookleafpub.com

ISBN: 9789360949846

First edition 2024

PREFACE

There's this conversation I had years ago that always replays in my mind. It's a conversation about lightning bugs, you know, the little flying bugs with lights on their butts. The bugs we used to chase after as kids and watch in awe. We would run into the house asking anybody who would listen for a jar, picking grass out the yard and poking holes in the lid, making a nice little home. We would try to catch them and put them in the jar, watching them light up. Hoping to keep them forever. They never told us how detrimental this was for them. We put grass in the jar but we really didn't know what they ate or what they needed. Putting Lightning Bugs in a jar is such a selfish act. It's all about us and wanting to keep something that isn't meant to be kept. This conversation I had years ago was a comparison to women and lightning bugs. It was a discussion about those who see something beautiful or mesmerizing and their initial thought is to capture it. They don't truly know what you need or if they even have the capabilities to provide it, but they want to keep you. They may even lose interest in you and put you away on top of a dresser, forcing your light to go out while locked inside of a jar. This book is a collection of thoughts on Lightning Bugs and a reminder to never let them catch you. I hope your light shines forever Little Lightning Bug.

Sincerely,

A Lightning Bug

Hey You!

Hey Little Lightning Bug!

Be careful they might catch you

Make sure you don't get too close

They have these little jars they like to put you in
and keep you forever

The jars have a little food and they even poke
holes to help you breathe but it's not where you
want to be

Little Lightning Bug, you'll surely die in there

You belong free

You're supposed to fly high, shining your light
all over the world.

Don't let them catch you Little Lightning Bug,
stay far away

Don't let that beautiful light of yours die out, the
world needs it.

Lurking Around

It's almost like they can smell it
They can smell your innocence
They can sense a pure heart and ingenuous mind
They become intrigued by those big, wide eyes
They stand from a distance and watch you,
mouth watering
They try to clean themselves for you, wiping
away the blood of their last victim
Trying to disguise the scent of the ones before
you
Stuffing their claws into gloves
They start slow, walking around you as if they
have their own reason for being there
They strike up conversation, as if they have a
genuine interest
They've mastered the art of gaining a person's
trust, being everything you need them to be
But what they don't know is, you've been down
this road before
They watched you from a distance and never
saw your scars
They don't know that you saw them before they
saw you
They didn't realize they missed a stain on the
top of their shoe

The scent of the pure isn't something you can
just cover up, especially to one of the same kind
Their snarl can't help but appear when they talk
But you continue on, as if you see nothing
Just an unaware, naive prey
Waiting for their strike
Because you know they will and when they do,
You simply turn the predator into the prey

Falling Out Of Love With Love

I'm falling out of love with love
Where's everything they promised
And why do I have to compromise, can't I have
it all
I used to be so optimistic about love, so excited
Now, I'm completely indifferent about it
Love was supposed to be the cure all, the healer
and reliever
Instead, its feeling like a burden and another
thing I need an escape from
I want to get back to a childlike belief in love
The belief that love is magical
I want to be delusional about love

You mustn't Forget

Don't forget about your light
Sometimes we do get stuck in a jar
Sometimes we fly into the jar not realizing its a
trap
When we do, we sink to the bottom thinking
how badly of a mistake we just made
You can't let your mind fall victim to where
your body lies
Your light is your light no matter where it is
Your light will shine wether its out flying high or
stuck in a jar
That light is your guide
Though it may seem impossible, it can lead you
out of anything
It can lead you to heights you never thought
were possible

Side Effects of Loneliness May Include:

Depression

Self Doubt

Desperation

Loss of Humor

A Lack of Creativity

A Doubt of Aspirations

The Seeking of Attention

A Deeper Fall into Solitude

Misery

Anxiety

Passive Agression

Thoughts of Self-Harm

If you're experiencing any of these symptoms
please reach out to someone as soon as possible.
Just because you feel lonely doesn't mean you
are alone.

Reciprocity

I called you because you were on my mind
You called me because you thought I was with
someone else and your ego wanted to see if I'd
pick up

I praise you because I admire who you are as a
person
You love bomb me because you want me in your
pocket

I openly share my thoughts and feelings because
this space feels safe
You strategically tell me what you want me to
know and make sure I never find out what you
don't

Your playing chess
And I'm waiting for the game to be over

I want to spend time with you
You want me to want to spend time with you

I want to hear everything that's on your mind
You hold everything in

I have all the hope there is for the future
You're barely making it through the day

Your going through this relationship in survival
mode

Passing Through

Have you ever experienced a relationship that is
bound by nothing
A relationship that is completely selfless
It's no give and take but just a give
Nothing is expected
Just the simple enjoyment of company and
conversation
Some people wish to hold you hostage and keep
you forever
Some people give in order to receive
Some people seek companionship and will find
it in whoever is available
But this relationship is a pure one
An unspoken bond wrapped in an endless
amount of trust
When we connect its an outpour of thoughts,
feelings, ideas and everything in between
And when it's time to go, we both pack our
selves up and continue on
Bound by nothing
Held by nothing
Just a mutual respect and admiration

Fire

Sometimes a cleanse isn't always with water
Sometimes it's fire and it burns
Sometimes it's destructive
It's hot and unbearable
It destroys everything and leaves nothing to be
salvaged
It's the ultimate cleanse
It's the cleanse you would have never done
The changes you would've never made
It's the push you needed to truly transform

Let's Talk

I could sit and talk with you for hours
I want to hear it all
Let's talk about life and love
Peace and pain
Heartaches and heartbreaks
Tragedies and triumphs
Let's contemplate
Let's figure life out
Let's wonder and wish
And to be clear this is not a love poem
Because conversation is not restricted to lovers
Conversation is a bond builder
It's a wall breaker
Conversation is a relieve for those who need it
A conversation is an answer to your question
It's an ease to your worry
So let's talk, and bring some peace to our minds
Let's spend the day, drifting away, getting lost in
conversation.

Must I Remind You

Must I remind you, there is no ceiling
You can fly away at any time and go chase the
world
You can do the unthinkable
The unimaginable are the visions you see for
yourself everyday
There is no limit when it comes to you

The Choice Is Yours

Choose happiness
Choose love
Choose peace
Choose tranquillity
Choose honesty
Choose to reside in your power
Choose to encourage
Choose to motivate
Choose growth
Choose courage
Choose balance
Choose to enlighten
Choose faith
Choose hope
Choose trust
Choose all that good

The Ying and The Yang

I hope my feminine makes you want to get in
your masculine as your masculine makes me
want to get in my feminine

I hope the essence of my name sings to you as
yours does to me

I hope the sound of my voice slowly wraps
around your ears and travels through you the
same way yours travels through me

I hope my femininity serves as a soft cushion for
you to rest upon because your masculine is a
fortified castle in which I feel safe to reside

I hope I do to you what you do to me

I hope I give you what you give me

Magic

There's a special type of magic about her
It's something that just pulls you in
There's no tricks or spells
Just an essence and an aura that is simply
undeniable
She is the magic
She is the spell
Her eyes
Her words
The sound of her voice
Her touch
Her skin
Her energy

Jarred Dreams

To not pursue an interest is like holding a brick
of hot coal in your hands.

It becomes so intense to the point where it
destroys you.

When you hold onto a dream given to you, your
soul dies a little.

That dream sits in you and rot

It festers and begins to stink

There's this feeling of un-doneness

A feeling of un-fulfillment

There's a hole in your chest where that dream is
supposed to be

It is imperative to go after every dream

It is important to leave no stone unturned on this
earth

You allow those dreams to sit dormant

You become miserable

You die before your death

The Destroyers

As much love and admiration as your light
attracts

As many people who watch in awe when you
shine

There are many who see you and seek to destroy
you

They see your light and want to take it

Either for themselves or simply because they
don't want you to have it

Fly high little lightning bug and avoid the
destroyers at all cost

Sometimes they play nice, sometimes they don't

Sometimes their intentions are obvious,
sometimes they're hidden

Trust yourself and what you feel

How Are You?

How are you really?

What's burdening you?

What's keeping you up at night?

What's on your mind?

What's frustrating you?

I know the feeling

To be okay when you're not okay

Let this be safe place

A place that doesn't require you to pretend

A place where you can truly answer

So once again I ask,

How are you really?

Silence

I used to be scared of silence
It chased me my whole life
I ran from it every chance I got
I looked for noise, distractions
Anything to break the silence
But in silence I found peace
I found wisdom
I found possibility and inspiration
Like a friend refusing to leave you in your time
of need, silence stayed with me
It was constant in my life
And no matter how much I ran from it, it always
found me
Especially in the times when I needed out the
most
It knew that it was a necessity in my life, even
when I didn't

To Catch A Lightning Bug

To catch a lightening bug, it takes skill

You have to know that they begin to appear in the evening

You see one random flicker of light then the rest start to join in

After a while you realize, early evening is when they feel safe to come out and shine

Like any other bug, they're slightly wary of swift movements

It takes a calm steady hand

To catch a lightning bug takes a bit of tricky and slight deception

You have to catch them when they're distracted

You fool them with the idea of a safe space

A space that has all they think they would need

To catch a lightning bug is to destroy them

It's to take away their freedom and render them
useless

It's to make them question themselves, their
abilities and their decision making

When you catch a lightning bug, they are no
longer lightning bugs

The light that you loved so much slowly begins
to fade and eventually goes out

To catch a lightning bug is to deprive the world
of the light it so desperately needs

9 789360 949846